TABLE OF CONTENTS

INTRODUCTION

Becoming financially independent has to do with first knowing, and accepting, the rules of wealth. Believe it or not, early retirement is possible when you learn how to become financially independent. Yes, even in today's economy. I hear of folks all the time making $20,000 a month and above. And, in my opinion, the real "security" is in establishing a system with a real residual income formula for whether you roll out of bed or roll over in bed in the morning. To me, this makes far more sense than accumulating a large sum of money in the bank. Because who's to say how long you're going to live?

Reaching the parallax of wealth creation is like reaching the top of a hard mountain. However with innovative methods and a shift in mindset, the once hard trek to the top becomes a fair trip with paved roads. Equipping ourselves with the right techniques in wealth building will make tall orders turn into silly hurdles.

However, people mistake that creating wealth is a trivial matter. People wrongly assume that a few wise investments and a lot of hard work will make them happy campers. However, after retirement, they find themselves wanting to go back to their working years once again. People thereby tend to underestimate the journey of building wealth.

Becoming financially independent begins with your mindset...

Of all the rules of wealth, the most important rule of becoming financially independent is your mindset. Look around you. You'll see that the wealthy people who can buy whatever they want have no fear whatsoever of how they're going to pay for it.

Consider Robert Kiyosaki, given a chance to make 2 billion dollars but he only had 1 billion in reserve. Do you think he'd say, "I can't do that, it's beyond my budget"? No way, he'd find a way to get the extra money so he could start making more money! Average people ask "how much does it cost" while wealthy people ask "how much can I make".

I like to listen on a daily basis to You Tube training videos that lift me up to a better wealthier mindset. Did you ever notice that wealthy people tend to hang together? It's actually a fact that your income is dictated as the average income of five of your closest friends.

I don't advocate being judgmental or superficial when you pick your friends, but I find that when you think more of yourself with a better self-image, you will attract wealthier and more stable people around you, which pushes you up as well.

Becoming financially independent from your home computer...

Now, let's get down to nuts and bolts. With the idea that you want to build a passive residual income from home, which is the smartest way to becoming financially independent, you need to establish a way to make contact with the world who will be sending you money.

Gone are the days of door-to-door marketing and cold calling, since nobody's ever home during the day and people will invariably always have their caller ID on to screen calls. So I guess we can agree that online marketing is where it's at, especially if your intention is "becoming financially independent" from home.

But what about becoming financially independent "from scratch" when you don't know anything about internet marketing?

Fun is all in learning how to become financially independent...

Yes, if that's you, I have an answer for you, too! There are many people in the network marketing industry who've made it big online! But you have to start out with a system that not only pays well but will train you and work with you step by step. You can even check out the MLM alternative with online marketing.

The thing you need to remember is that the sky's the limit. So many of us "get in our own way" by believing that we are only worth "$X" amount of dollars. You're worth it, so believe it... you can do it!

Get Bonus Materials: https://growwealthy.lpages.co/blueprint/

WEALTH RULE #1

The universal reality that you get to keep a part of everything that you earn in life, when you understand it, can make you genuinely rich. In concept, this sounds bad, because it seems like you are paying most of what you earn and keeping very little of what is earned. But, in reality, if you use that part correctly, you can ultimately earn much more if you simply understand the full import of that universal reality that you keep for yourself or benefit from a part of what you earn.

The part you keep gets bigger as you use it better! As you genuinely grow, all areas benefit, including your positive income and spending capacity. If you try to keep all that you earn, you use it up much quicker and cannot renew anything because you do not invest what you keep and increase your capacity for action and growth.

The fact that we usually start small and slow and become big and fast, should tell us something definitive. What it tells us all is that we must build rationally and work steadily. Also, when it is given to us it is easier to use up and deplete because we do not learn the process of how to make more.

"Teach a man to go fishing in the lake and cook it himself, he eats for life. Give a man a cooked fish, he eats for a few minutes."

Personal wealth building basics start with getting more value out of what you already have. Do you ever feel like you're putting money into a purse (or wallet) that has holes in it? If so, you've probably wished for an increase in income more than once. However, what if instead you could keep more of what you're earning? As you can imagine, accomplishing this first would help you be confident that earning more money will be a positive experience instead of just having more to lose.

Here are some personal wealth building habits that will help you keep more of the money that you're already earning...

Personal Wealth Building Starts With Awareness

Getting control of the money you're already making and getting the most value out of it starts with awareness. For one month, do nothing but keep track of your income and your outgo. Track everything from the money that you pay for your mortgage to the money that you spend on coffee every morning. Control begins with awareness, and the best way to become aware of your current financial situation is to get a clear picture of your life in front of you on paper based on a month of your spending habits.

"Spend less than you earn until you are able to earn more than you spend"

Umm, that is an interesting thought, (Spend less than you earn until you are able to earn more than you spend). In other words, do not spend what you do not have. Do not live off credit or borrowed money. Learn to live off 80% of your net income. Also do not quit your current JOB. Listed below is an outline to help you achieve financial success NOW!

Here Are The Five Money Streams For Long-Term Wealth Building.

1. **Job** - don't quite your day job. This part is the most guaranteed.
2. **Residual Income** - affiliates and partners.
3. **Small Business Income** - on/off line stores.
4. **Investment Payouts** - Forex, Stocks, Bank Interest, and investments.
5. **Rental Property Income** - Flats or small apartments, commercial build.

Now, here is where you must do your homework and see what works for you and your family. Wealth is building a system to provide a steady stream of income to you and your loved ones. Please and I do mean please, don't quiet your current JOB, until your business is earning at least what your current job pay is + an additional 25% of your gross job income(this will cover health insurance/taxes)+ 12 months of your monthly living expenses in the bank.

Apply the Four Bucket Personal Finance System

The four bucket personal finance system is a simple system for reprioritizing your spending according to what will add value to your life and maximize the income you already have. With this system, you organize your spending according to four categories:

1. **Investing**: 5% or more of your monthly income.
2. **Expenses**: 80% or less of your monthly income.
3. **Cash Reserves**: 5% or more of your monthly income.
4. **Giving**: 10% or more of your monthly income.

Investing would be money you're spending on increasing personal wealth, investing in the stock market or building a dream (such as starting your own business). Expenses are the things which you need to survive, your standard monthly bills. Cash reserves is the money that you're setting aside for planned purchases or saving for emergencies. Finally, tithing or charitable contributions are the final 10% of your income.

The order and percentage of these four buckets is key, because it helps you to make investing a priority. Wealthy people always make investing a priority, and the more you do this, the more value you'll get out of what you already have.

Save no less than 5% of what you earn. Following this rule will cause your wallet to fatten over time. So get started with these simple personal wealth building habits right now. Within a year, you'll be well on your way to creating financial freedom.

WEALTH RULE #2

BUDGET YOUR EXPENSES

If you do not budget yourself, there is no way of achieving financial freedom. When you decide to budget yourself, you have to keep track of all your income from different sources and above all you keep a track on your expenses. Once you manage to keep track of your expenses, you become aware of how much you are spending on unnecessary things.

Writing out a budget does not create a burdensome restraint. A budget is a template for you to follow and assist you with establishing good spending habits.

In the beginning when you start budgeting your expenses, it could be quite difficult and boring. However, once you realize the importance of budgeting, you automatically relish the idea of budgeting. You have to budget yourself in order to reach your financial goals. Come on, even big and small businesses do it.

When you decide to budget your expenses you will start controlling them. You will resist from spending money uselessly and you will even pay your bills on time to avoid being slapped with a late fee penalty. Budgeting will help to improve your credit rating as you will no longer be defaulting on your loan payments. You will also end up saving more money which you can divert to different investment vehicles to increase your net worth after a period of time.

So budgeting is important but first you need to start the budgeting process. List down all sources of your income. This includes salary, dividends, interests and rents from property owned by you. You can check out your recent tax return form to find out all the sources of your income if you are not sure what qualifies as income.

Once you finish doing this, prepare a list of your expenses. This will include items like grocery, mortgage, utility bills, transportation, credit card bills, house repairs, life insurance, entertainment and anything else you spend your money on.

Then figure out where you can cut down on unnecessary expenses and stick to that decision. You have to make sure that 5 percent of your gross income is always directed to your savings. If you do not start saving, you will not benefit from budgeting your expenses.

You can do a monthly budget and stick to it. It does require self discipline but the benefits are immense in the long run.

Is the thought of putting a budget together similar to your thoughts about having a root canal done? If so, you aren't alone. If you've never put one together before, or have never felt the need to operate under one, it can seem like a very daunting task. But in reality, budgets aren't all that hard to devise and put into use. When you get used to them, and understand the significant value a budget has when you take your future into consideration, you'll be very happy you sat down and put one together.

There are three steps you'll need to go through when putting a budget together.

1. Categorizing Your Expenses
2. Estimating What You Spend
3. Calculating And Adjusting

When you begin the process of setting up a budget, you'll start by setting up your larger categories first, then you'll break them down into smaller expense categories. Here's a great list of categories to begin with:

Housing
Mortgage or rent payments, repairs, property taxes, cleaning supplies, homeowners or tenants insurance, utilities, furniture and decor.

Food
Groceries, meals that you eat out, pizza delivery, snacks and drinks at work

Transportation
Any expenses that have to do with you car or transportation to work, including car payments, insurance, gas oil, parking, repairs, and public transportation costs

Medical Expenses
Insurance premiums, insurance deductibles, out of pocket expenses, eye care, dental care, pharmacy

Clothing
New clothes, dry cleaning, repairs

Personal Expenses
Makeup, hair care, shampoo, conditioners, etc.

Insurance
Life Insurance, Umbrella insurance, and any other insurance not covered in the other categories

Education
Tuition, dues and fees, school photos, yearbooks, school supplies and books

Credit Accounts
Payments on credit cards, department store cards, lines of credit through your bank, credit union or other loans, any other outstanding debts you may have

Gifts
For various holidays, birthdays, graduations, weddings, showers, etc.

Recreation
Vacations, movies, books, magazines, newspapers, cable TV, restaurants, sporting events, sporting registration fees, sports equipment, coaches gifts

Donations
Church and charity donations

You'll also need to set aside funds each month for the yearly and quarterly payments that you'll run into. These payments have a habit of sneaking up on you when you are least prepared for them. Don't forget to include these in your budget. Things like tax payments, water bills, and so on. Just divide the total figure by 12 and include them into your budget.

Within each category above, you'll see that some of the sub categories are essential, such as the mortgage or rent payment, the electric and grocery line item. But, you'll also see that some are not essential. Things like furniture, the gift line item and having pizza delivered.

Your task now will be to divide your general categories into two sub categories - essential and non essential expenses. Only you will know what's essential to your situation. Perhaps you need to eat out 5 nights a week due to your job. Or, maybe you need to buy new clothes more often than the normal person due to your job. The point is that you'll need to think long and hard about your essential and non essential expenses. Only you will really know what is a must have and a not so must have. Be honest with yourself.

As you divide up your expenses into the two lists, look through both of them to find items that you can be flexible with. Things like clothing, groceries and other food related expenses that you may be able to cut back on. Put a star next to these items you can be flexible with.

These flexible budget items are where you are going to be able to key in on in order to save some money. Sure, you'll always have to pay your water bill, but perhaps you can cut back on your cable TV package - or eliminate all together.

Desires increase with income, so don't confuse your desires with necessary expenses.

Get Bonus Materials: https://growwealthy.lpages.co/blueprint/

WEALTH RULE #3

PUT YOUR SAVINGS TO WORK

MOST OF US LOVE MONEY. And when the bills arrive, we love it even more when we know we have the power to spend it. And most of us do actually plan before spending it. But somehow, we often find ourselves getting a shock, like when the balance of the bank statement shows an incredible amount of money debited. And you probably don't know where to, unless you had the presence of mind to record all your spending. It is true that many of us enjoy planning. But not planning your finances well is like seeking the inevitable "poverty"- pockets left dry and with huge financial deficit, too. In the end you will find yourself withdrawing much more than you have deposited.

The best thing to do with money now is to invest it wisely. The most important reason for investing money is to generate wealth. Wealth that you could use to finance your long-term goals like education or retirement. Whatever avenue of investment you choose you will be surprised at how quickly your small savings will multiply to create great wealth.

There are three critical questions that you must ask yourself when considering a potential investment opportunity:

1) Is my original investment secure?
2) What is my return on investment(ROI), AND, potential loss?
3) How knowledgeable am I or my advisor on this particular investment?

Investing Wisely

Though you may be completely convinced about the benefits of investing, you may want to proceed with some caution before you start investing. Avoid the common mistakes that most people make regarding their investments by using the following tips.

- **Do not sit on your savings.** While there is no assurance that investing in the market or other plans will give you a guaranteed return, not investing is not an option. If you are serious about growing your money, you have to be serious about investing.

- **Start now.** If you have made up your mind about investing, then postponing will cause you to lose out on the returns that your money may be earning even as you are dilly-dallying.

- **Do not invest before all debt is cleared.** While it may be tempting to invest the money you have in your savings account in some attractive plan in the market, if you have debt still left unpaid on your credit card then you are not investing wisely. For example, suppose you are still left with a debt of $2000 on your credit card and you have exactly $2000 in your savings account. If you are tempted to withhold payment and invest in the market instead, you will first of all have to bear an interest burden of anywhere from 18% to 24% on the outstanding debt. This also means that your investment after paying taxes has to have a minimum return of anywhere from 18% to 24% just to break even. This is quite a risk to take. First pay off all your debts and only then think of investing.

- **Never invest for short term unless.** We should correct that to say that you should invest your money in the short-term if you require it immediately in the short-term. However, investing money in the stock market works out well only if you are willing to play the waiting game and do not need the money for at least the next three to five years. On the other hand if you need to invest money for just a short period needing it soon for buying a new car or for a family vacation, then put your money in short term plans, like trading stocks.

- **Use your 401(k) well.** Some employers now match any contribution that you make to your 401(k) up to a certain percentage of your salary. Use this well by putting in the maximum allowed contribution to the fund thereby forcing your employer to do the same.

- **Be prepared to take risks.** When you are young, you should be investing most of your savings in the stock market, as you have enough time on your side to be able to ride out any ups and downs in the market and enjoy long-term gains. As the years go by, you may want to slowly move some of the funds into bonds.

- **Do not be a daredevil.** While the market always favors the brave, you do not have to be foolhardy and invest in instruments you know nothing about. Never invest in a plan that could come to naught.

- **Staying Invested.** As we have already mentioned the best investing plan is to make a careful study of all the options open to you, select the one best suited to your purpose and then stay invested for the long-term. Trading in and out of the market will only result in fees being charged every time you do so and you will miss out on the gains of long-term investment.

If you are convinced of the benefits of investing and would like to put in your savings in an investment vehical, it is time to look at the various investment vehicals and see how each one compares.

Obviously the single determining factor would be the rate of return you would get on the investment that you are making. While long-term investments offer the best rates of returns, at times, you may want to invest even in small term vehicals though they may not offer such great returns.

After making money your slave, make its children your slave, and it's children's children your slave.

Get Bonus Materials: https://growwealthy.lpages.co/blueprint/

WEALTH RULE #4

SEEK OUT, WORK WITH & EMPLOY WISE ADVISORS

True wealth advisors ensure that you and your family are free from financial worries for a lifetime. The political and economic conditions of the country are fast changing. At times of crisis, investors get worried about their investments and make hasty decisions which may cause hefty losses. Your wealth advisers guide you in times of investment turbulance.

When you have a wealth manager, you need not worry about anything in the world. Choose private wealth managers who have ample experience and expertise. A good wealth advisor tries to understand your financial circumstances, and then gives you an evaluation of the best available options. These wealth solutions are customized to suit your individual needs. The advisors also file taxes and help you grow your assets over a period of time. They offer advice in a family stewardship style and keep everyone together so all can enjoy a good lifestyle.

Good experiences with friends, church, community, and financial security enrich our lives. At times of emotional crisis, one tends to make snap decisions about wealth. If you are divorced or going through a divorce it is a good idea to secure your wealth in a long term investment. A good wealth advisor will give you both moral support and work with your attorney to ensure you get your righteous share and invest it in an intelligent way. One can also gather more information from the internet but it is always wise to hire an experienced advisor who will ensure you have true wealth.

For the people in the know, social and philanthropic assets prove to be the best source of true wealth. When you have won the lottery or have written a million-seller book, there is money in the bank that is not being used in a profitable manner. Building a relationship with a true wealth advisor will help you secure your wealth from any events of the unforeseen and also help it grow. Learn the many streams of income that are low risk and suit your lifestyle. Online educational projects bring handsome returns these days. But make sure you invest in something you value and can adapt to easily. These same values and virtues will be passed down to your next generations.

Scheduling your annual Business Plan is a key activity for successful investment advisors and an essential task for your wealth to improve and grow year to year. A familys growth of wealth is contingent upon conscious and strategic action.

Amassing Wealth

In order to accumulate substantial wealth, you'll have to select riskier investments than you would otherwise. A rule of thumb is: the higher the risk, the higher the return. Of course, you could also lose money with riskier investments. It's wise to decide how much risk you feel comfortable with and communicate this to your financial planner. Working with a fee-based planner assures you that your planner isn't focused on commissions. Instead, you will pay for his or her services on an hourly basis. It's important to diversify your investments in order to protect your money. This is another way of saying: don't put all your eggs in one basket. You want to have some safe pools of money and some in riskier investments.

Short and snappy

Unless your plan is for an extreamly large family, you need not write a lengthy plan to get the benefits of strategic planning. Write a plan that is concise and to the point - one that contains the sections necessary to take conscious action. Two pages are generally all that is needed. I suggest writing optional pages to go along with your two page plan if you would like a more thorough plan. Plans that are too long are not used. Additions to your mini plan could be a mission statement and a target goal-these are important but not as essential as planning out your strategies and implementation activities - the key elements to success.

Plan to grow?

How do you want to grow your familys wealth in the coming year?

Finally, Only take advice on matters from people that are proven experts on the subject.

Free advice usually costs you the most!

Why on Earth would you seek advice about investing in real estate from a professional car dealer.

You'll make some bad judgement calls in the beginning, and you'll make some mistakes, and when you do, tell yourself, NEVER AGAIN!

Failures are the tolls you pay on the road to success.

Heres a proverb: Fool me once, shame on you,, fool me twice,, SHAME ON ME!

CAUTION!,,,,,no matter how tempting an opportunity may seem,,,NEVER risk more than you can afford to lose. The penalty of too much risk is probable loss.

Get Bonus Materials: https://growwealthy.lpages.co/blueprint/

WEALTH RULE #5

OWN YOUR HOME(HOMES)

Real estate Investments are an important part to every wealthy person's portfolio,,,Here's Why,,,,No matter what happens in your other businesses, you'll always have passive income (money you don't work for) streaming in from your real estate holdings.

There was a time when owning your own property was the ultimate goal. Having a home to call your own came with a sense of accomplishment, pride and security that was unmatched by anything else in life. As an added bonus to the 'feel good' aspect of home ownership was the fact that buying property was a sound investment move as national housing prices rose annually for more than 60 consecutive years.

In 2017 close to 27 million homeowners owed more than their homes were worth, and the numbers of foreclosures are rapidly increasing. With these types of numbers, is owning your home really such a good idea? Owning a home is still a priority for many Americans; however, it is no longer considered a safe asset class in regards to being an investment.

In 1945, real estate in the nation was positioned with a balance of 15.9% debt vs. 84.1% equity. By 2005 the debt ratio had risen to 40.1%, and by 2009 that figure had skyrocketed to 61%. According to these figures 'pride in ownership' seems to be the only benefit from owning your own home and it is no surprise that almost half of the population no longer believe that owning a home is a way of building wealth.

For some, the allure of home ownership goes beyond an investment opportunity, as one homeowner states, "I never looked at my primary residence as an investment. I wanted a place to live, and I didn't want to rent from someone else, so buying a home fulfilled those needs. And it's probably safe to assume that 30 years from now I could sell it for a profit, but of course I would be right back at the beginning with no place to live so it really is more of an expense than an investment anyway". This homeowner will likely enjoy many years in her home, and so long as she is comfortable with her mortgage payments, fluctuations in the market will have no affect on her.

For the more financially conscientious, or should I say uptight, this type of thinking is unheard of. To them real estate is an investment; and investments need returns. These are the folks that are joining the ever-increasing ranks of homeowners who are walking away from their 'bad investments'.

3 Ways Owning a Home Helps Families

There is no question that home ownership is one of the cornerstones of American society. That white picket fence flashes through the mind of most every potential home buyer at some point or another. We all dream of the big backyard with the shade tree and a big porch swing. But how does owning a home really help a family?

Reason #1

One big reason that owning a home is important to a family is the ability to generate future wealth. While this might not be the first thing a buyer thinks of, by choosing the right property for the right price they will later reap the rewards of equity. Investing in a home is rarely a mistake, especially if you get a good deal on the front end. Buyers never want to pay top dollar for a home, however.

Reason #2

Another reason owning a home is important is because families need roots. Families with children really need to have a home atmosphere where a child can grow up, develop long lasting friendships and make memories.

Reason #3

There are also important tax considerations when buying a home such as the tax deduction an owner gets for paying mortgage interest throughout the year. This can be a huge advantage for many people when they get their taxes done each year.

Building a strong family requires having a good foundation, and what could be better than your own home? Why continue paying rent to a landlord? Each month as you scratch out that rent check, you are helping that landlord pay down their mortgage. Why not write a check and start paying yourself back with equity? By investing in a home of your own, you are really paying yourself in the end. Every time you pay that mortgage payment, you will know that you are putting equity away for your future and your family's future.

Home ownership is the key to wealth in America.

Paying rent for 30 years leaves you owning Nothing,,,,Paying on a mortgage for 30 years leaves you owning a house Free & Clear!

Not many other things satisfies the spirit like being the Lord of your land (Landlord).

Build your wealth foundation out of Home Ownership,,,,,,WHY,,,,,because Real estate will always be there to catch you and help you bounce back!

Get Bonus Materials: https://growwealthy.lpages.co/blueprint/

WEALTH RULE #6

PLAN FOR YOUR FUTURE

We would all like to know that our family's financial future is secure especially in a difficult economy like ours.

But when you think about it, how safe is your family's future right now?

How can you tell?

You do only have one family and it is your responsibility to secure their financial future. The financial future of your family is dependent on what preparation you make for them in terms of life insurance, as well as in other ways. They would be well looked after if you should suddenly die, become disabled, or lose your job.

Steps to Take to Secure their Future
There are a few steps that you could do to help make this happen.

1. You have to set in place your long-term and short-term financial goals.
   - The question you do need to ask yourself is whether you do have a financial plan in place, and that includes life insurance.
   - If not, it is important that you look at what your expenditure is at present.
   - Make a list of all your income - that is, all the moneys that are coming in, but especially the regular income.
   - Make a list of all your expenditure - debts and living expenses.
   - Assess what you want your lifestyle to be from now until you retire.
   - Include in this planning, what your expectancy is of your children's education.

2. Once you have completed this assessment, you need to have a look at how you are going to achieve the financial goals for your family.
3. You would want to set up a program to get to the end goal, and this would include setting up insurance against any financial loss before you reach your goal.
4. This means that you have to take out a life insurance that would cover your loss of income, loss of life an even the loss of assets.
5. Should you pass on, this could take a huge chunk out of the pay out of your insurance as well.
6. You should try to shrink your credit and not fall into the traps again.
7. If you can, pay your mortgage off earlier by paying more than the premium if you can. Some banks have a linked savings account to which you can transfer these savings.
8. Credit always comes with interest and you should avoid this at all costs, because you are spending more than the initial cost of things.
9. It is important that you ensure that you take serious steps to prevent credit traps. If you can help yourself at all, do not make use of credit cards at all.
10. It is important that you draw up a will as well. This will ensure that your assets will be made available to your family immediately and not have a long waiting period.

These are only a few ways in which you can secure your family's future. There are many other simple daily tips that would assist you to ensure that your family have all they need when you are no longer around to help them. It is never too late to start managing your own finances in such a way that it would benefit you as well as your family. If you are not able to do so, many businesses are available that would be able to help you do so. The important thing is that you have a plan in place for the future.

Here are another 3 areas that you can check – and if you can strengthen these, you can more guarantee that your family will be financially strong for years to come.

1. Inflation.

In 1980 a stamp cost only 15 cents. Now its up to 55 cents. That's about a 300% increase in 30 years.

Inflation will eat away at whatever money you have - which means in the future, you will only be able to buy a fraction of the things you can buy now.

The inflation rate is currently averaging about 2-3% - if your money isn't earning more than that - then you are losing your money little by little every year.

Tip: invest your money to earn returns that are greater than the inflation rate, (a bank won't cut it) so that your money will grow to meet your family's future needs.

2. Taxes

Many of us are preparing for retirement by investing in a 401K, or IRA. Its a great strategy -especially if your employer matches your investment.

Unfortunately, if this is your only source for retirement - when the the time comes to pull it out, you may have a tax time bomb on your hands.

This is because the money in most qualified accounts (401K, 403b, IRAs, etc.) are taxable as ordinary income, when the money comes out.

Tip: find other tax free sources to invest your money into - such as a ROTH IRA or a life insurance policy where you can borrow from tax free.

When the time comes for you to get money out, take your money from all three sources so that you can keep your taxable income at a minimum. This will keep you in a lower tax bracket.

3. The 3 deadly "Ds"

Death, Disability and Disease.

These three things, though scary - are common to us as we grow older in age.

But, can you imagine what would happen to your family financially if any of these inevitable situations were to happen?

Are you and your family ready for it?

Tip: Insure yourself and your family against all three of these with sufficient life insurance, disability insurance - and long term care insurance.

Do it now, when its cheaper. Also do it now, because if you were to get sick, it will be much more expensive...or God forbid, no longer available to you.

Now, these are only a few of the challenges that need to be overcome in order to secure a better life for your family.

But if you conquer these, you can better guarantee a great financial future for your family, and know with confidence that you and your family will prosper in the years to come.

I guarantee you that the future consists of two possible outcomes, one with you here, or one without you here,,,,and you need a contingency plan for both possible outcomes!

A friend of mine likes to LBVS(laughing but very seriously) say, "When I retire I'm going to be on a FIXED income,,,BUT I'LL BE THE ONE FIXING IT!!-Nick

During your best working and income generating years is when you should be planning your retirement age and your monthly income throughout your retirement.

The best way to secure a future income for your family is by building your passive income.

There are three types of income:

1) Earned income. This type of income is from a job and is called 50% money, because after all the taxes are taken out your only left with 50% of what you earned.

2) Portfolio income. This type of income is from paper assets such as stocks, bonds, mutual funds............

This is called 80% money, because you will always pay 20% taxes on this type of income.

3) Passive income. This is income generated from real estate or a business that runs without you physically being there. This type of income is called 100% money, because you receive 100% of the money generated and through proper planning determine how much taxes you will pay, if any.

Get Bonus Materials: https://growwealthy.lpages.co/blueprint/

WEALTH RULE #7

BUILD A BUSINESS

A job will pay your bills, but building a business can make you wealthy!

You can't get wealthy trading your hours for dollars,, mainly because earned income(W2 income) is so heavily taxed and you're never in the driver's seat to control what you're worth.

On a job, the difference between what you are paid and what you're worth is called "your employer's profit" There's absolutely nothing wrong with working a job, if you're working with a vision!

The back-breaking working days of a person working with a vision is limited, but the back-breaking working days of a person working without a vision are endless.

A lot of people still believe that building a successful business depends only on tools or money and ignore the entrepreneurial mindset. That's why 3% of the people make more money than the other 97 % people on the planet. In order to get the results you want in business, the first step is to develop a new set of beliefs, attitudes and habits that can support you in this journey.

Have you ever wondered how the wealthiest people in the world originally built their fortunes? If you analyzed the Forbes 400 list of richest people in the United States, you'd find that more than 325 of them got on the list by applying a simple formula (or being the heir of someone who applied this formula).

What is this formula?

It's called a "business multiplier," and it's one of the greatest wealth leverage points of all time.

Let's explore the business multiplier concept by walking through the value of a fictitious business we'll call Star Biz, Inc. as it progresses through the normal stages and levels of a business's development.

Level One: Business Start-Up

Value: Zero

You probably already know that a business start-up is nothing more than an idea and a plan; as such, it has no value in the market. The only exception to this might be if the plan has intellectual property attached to it such as a patent that will be applied or a trade secret process that will be leveraged. So at Level One, the business value of our imaginary business, Star Biz, Inc., is zero.

Early Stage Level Two: Business Scrambling for Its Survival

Value: Very Little

At Early Stage Level Two, this business has few paying customers. It's desperately trying to secure more clients and fulfill its promises to them long enough to establish a secure base for the business.

At this stage, Star Biz, Inc. still has no real value other than that of its tangible assets, including its equipment, inventory, and fixtures (and even those won't be valued at more than a fraction of original cost), or some deeply discounted value of its current annual sales.

The valuation of most Early Stage Level Two businesses is the liquidation value of its hard assets.

Middle Stage Level Two: A Successful Business that Revolves Around the Owner

Gross Sales: $500,000

Net Profit: $150,000
Value: $150,000

Once Star Biz, Inc. has a consistent track record of generating profits, it gains value. But that value will be limited because the business depends on the owner being present and involved.

While every business has different valuation formulas, most owner-reliant Middle Stage Level Two businesses end up valued in the $50,000 to $500,000 range. The actual value will depend on the industry, the length of operating history, the value of its hard assets (e.g., inventory, equipment, etc.), and the sales volume of the business. But the biggest limitation to selling a Middle Stage Level Two business is its limited pool of buyers. Usually only mom-and-pop buyers will step into the owner's shoes and "own" their own jobs. Plus they have very little access to any large capital sources which limits what they can afford to pay.

With Star Biz, Inc., let's make these two assumptions: (1) It's a service business with a profit margin of 30 percent, meaning 30 cents out of every dollar of sales ends up as net profit. (2) Its gross sales are $500,000, which means the business nets $150,000 per year.

So in this hypothetical example, we're pegging the value of Star Biz, Inc. at $150,000, which is one times its annual net income.

Advanced Stage Level Two: A Successful Business Much Less Reliant on the Owner's Presence to Function

Gross Sales: $3.4 million
Net Profit: $1 million
Value: $3 million

Once Star Biz, Inc. hits Advanced Stage Level Two, it has key leaders employed in three of its core pillars. The business still benefits from the owner's leadership, but the company is becoming more systems-reliant every day. Sales are climbing fast. In fact, gross sales are $3.4 million dollars and net profit is $1 million per year.

While that $1 million profit sure feels good, even better is being an Advanced Stage Level Two business. At this stage, Star Biz, Inc. is now valued by a special formula called a business multiplier. The company is now valued at a multiple of its operating profit, which is a simplification but an accurate one. Every industry has its own range of business multipliers used in valuing a business in that industry.

Here's the best part. As you progress to Level Three, not only is your business more valuable because you're increasing both gross sales and operating profits, but you're also increasing the business multiplier that your business can command. For example, your business at Advanced Stage Level Two might only command a three or four times (3-4x) multiplier, but when you hit Level Three, you might command an eight or ten times (8-10x) multiplier.

In our example, at Advanced Stage Level Two we valued Star Biz, Inc. at three times (3x) its net profit, or $3 million. Let's see what happens when Star Biz, Inc. reaches Level Three.

Level Three: A Systems-Reliant Business with Winning Management Team in Place

Gross Sales: $10 million
Net Profit: $3 million
Value: $21 million

By this point, your Level Three business operates like a well-oiled machine. Your winning management team is in place, and your business controls and systems allow you to scale the business.

In our example, Star Biz, Inc. has grown its gross sales to $10 million, providing $3 million per year of net profit. As a Level Three business, Star

Biz, Inc. now commands a seven times (7x) business multiplier, pegging its value at seven times (7x) its net earnings, or $21 million.

Notice that sales at Star Biz, Inc. have grown by only 300 percent from when the business was an Advanced Stage Level Two business, but it's now worth seven times more. This demonstrates the multiplying power of leveraging a higher business multiplier. This is how business owners can build significant net worth fast.

Get Bonus Materials: https://growwealthy.lpages.co/blueprint/

WEALTH RULE #8

Acknowledge(Consider) God In All That You Do

Prosperous living requires taking a drive on the path to wealth. One of the primary shortcuts, in reaching your destination, involves acknowledging the true source of abundance-GOD.

There is only one true source in the universe that holds unlimited supply. God it the true source of all wealth; including financial wealth, spiritual and physical prosperity.

It is important to understand that when you acknowledge God as your source, temporary financial struggles no longer need to dictate your outcome. Why? Because, there are many ways and means that God can use to supply your needs. And His supply never runs dry.

God is the source and everyone else is His instrument. Many people make the mistake of thinking that their job is the source of their supply. But they need to realize that God is the source, and He simply uses their work as a means to let the funds flow to them.

"My God shall supply all your needs according to His riches." -- Philippians 4:19
Notice it says 'My God', not the company you work for. God is your source.
An Invisible Reservoir of Abundance

Norman Vincent Peale talks about an invisible reservoir of abundance in the universe. This is a great image of the abundance of God.

As we continually acknowledge God as the source of our supply, we'll find that we are divinely guided on our path to wealth. God is able to make a way when there seems to be no way. Realize it is our choice to recognize God's power and ownership over everything. And remember we are only stewards of what He supplies us.

Putting our faith and trust in a job, a person, or any other income source, has been proven to be a letdown at one time or another in life.

Prosperity is the result of our choice to accept and trust that God's ways are higher than ours. When we live by His ways, they will guide us on the path to wealth and allow us to tap into the invisible reservoir of abundance. We will then be like trees planted by rivers of water and prospering in everything we put our hand to. (**Psalm 1:3**)

Make no mistake about it: We will never go wrong acknowledging God as the source of our supply. However, be fair warned, if we choose not to, we can expect a lot of detours on our path to wealth.

May your eyes always be fixed on God as your source and may your life be filled with growing prosperity!

Trust in the LORD with all your heart, and do not rely on your own insight. In all your ways acknowledge him, and he will make straight your paths.

~Proverbs 3:5-6 (NRSV).

It's bound to be a great encouragement to learn that acknowledgment - as both a concept and method - is a thing that both confounds and controls the entire world, proving God's utter dominion.

Acknowledgment is truth. It's meeting truth. It's dealing in truth, choosing for it.

It is the preset of honesty and the willingness to see, hear and believe in truth.

To Be Bold or to Not Be Bold - Is That the Question?

There's nothing wrong with a quiet belief in God, but there is much gain to be had in living in acknowledgment. This is nothing about spruiking of God left, right and centre.

Instead it's about personifying the truth in all we do. Consequently, acknowledgment most majestically has its way with us and it is foreboding in our provision.

"To be bold or not be bold" is not really the right question. "To acknowledge or not acknowledge," then, is the right question.

Acknowledge.

Going Against the Grain of Our Default

Of course, it's here we start to recognise the gaps in our own levels of acknowledgment. We're ever so hard on ourselves at times. But we needn't stay in our default or get derailed to the burden of our pasts anchored there.

Acknowledging God is about acknowledging the truth all throughout life. It's living obediently. And though we cite plenty of examples where we've not done this so well, God's simply interested - for us - in our futures.

Living Acknowledgment

The rubber has to hit the road at some point.

Truth becomes humility when we exemplify acknowledgment, and this really does need to infiltrate our deeper lives.

For a moment's embarrassment or shame we shake off the shackles of guilt in a godly sleight of hand.

As we refuse to rely on our own insight, and more fully approach a God-imbued insight, we realise the blessings of living according to the actual design of life.

This is a concept that the world battles with; it cannot fully grasp it. The world belongs to acknowledgment and it cannot escape this wisdom of God's. It's inherent to life; a cord of grace prewired into the destiny of all creation.

Our acknowledgment of the power vested in acknowledgment is to us blessing.

It is a pure and simple, albeit very powerful, idea.

It is rather easy now to know just why we can overcome the world in our alignment with God, despite the refusal of the world to go God's way. (See **John 16:33**.)

For this, so far as a manner of living is concerned, the Christian way is a distinct and comprehensive advantage as we learn to lead in love.

The Creator thinks differently than creation. The best way to try to get a glimpse of God's point of view on a situation is by studying the Bible.

The Bible is full of Trues, Parables and Examples of other peoples experiences that you can draw from and shortcut your process to success.

This is my command—be strong and courageous! Do not be afraid or discouraged. For the Lord your God is with you wherever you go."
Joshua 1:8-9 NLT

CONCLUSION

I've always told my kids, whether you think you can or you think you can't, you're probably right! The same holds true for becoming truly wealthy. Unfortunately, most people NO LONGER believe it. Retirement confidence surveys show that only 37% of Americans believe that they can - or will - be rich someday. The other 63% have given up, doomed to a life of paycheck to paycheck living because they no longer believe a better financial future is possible. Don't get me wrong, I'm not saying that all you have to do is think it to be it (otherwise I'd be a professional basketball player by now). What I amsaying, is that you have to be ready - mentally - to transition from things that don't work (like what you've been doing) to things that do work (the things that the wealthy have done for hundreds of years).

It sounds like a no-brainer, but the truth is most people just aren't ready. Most people have been walking in the same circle for so long, that they've become comfortable in the rut they've been digging. And besides, doing nothing and complaining about your crappy situation is often easier than taking the necessary steps to make a change. Have you ever known a smoker who talked about quitting forever but failed every to quit every time they tried? It's easier to complain about the negatives of smoking than it is to do what it takes to quit. Frankly, no one eversucceeds at quitting until they have mentally decided that they WANT to quit. Becoming wealthy is the same way, unless you're ready you'll never succeed.

There are specific things you can do to get ready, to mentally prepare yourself, to make sure you WANT to be wealthy, but for now let's assume that you are indeed ready. Here are the top 5 things you must be prepared to do:

1. **Balance today's WANTS with tomorrow's NEEDS:** When opportunities present themselves, you need to be ready (mentally AND financially) to take advantage of them. Whether it be a great stock trade, chance to buy into a business, make a loan to someone or anything else that requires a little capital, either you have it OR you miss out. As much fun as driving a fancy car and eating out seems to be today, it does nothing for your financial future tomorrow.

2. Realize mistakes from the past (and learn from them): Doing what you've been doing and following the crowds has gotten you exactly where you are today. If you're not happy with where you are, you need to realize that the traditional financial wisdom you've been following NO LONGER WORKS! Truth be told, it never really worked for many people to begin with.

3. Be open to new ways of thinking: If the ideas you've been following haven't been working, it's time to listen to some new ones. Ideas that will lead you away from the crowd. Ideas that will teach you different methods that don't include the stock market or your 401(K). Ideas that remove taxes and lost interest payments from your future.

4. Be committed: It's time to use a little common sense and realize that unless you're lucky enough to win the lottery or sign a record deal, you won't get rich over night. It's simple math, it takes time and money (and the discipline to follow the 6 rules of wealth, of course) to build a future full of money. There is no get-rich-quick scheme that actually works.

5. Change you're thinking from money out, to money in: With very little effort you can change the flow of money in your life from money out (payments to banks and credit cards), to money in (payments from all sorts of places being made to you). If you collect money from other - or from yourself - instead of letting others collect money from you, your finances will be transformed.

You've tried things your way. Now it's time to stop staying up at night worrying about your 401(K) and the stock market. It's time to stop following the masses and take the steps to KNOW that your future is secure. No matter how far down life's road you've travelled, if you find you are going the wrong way the time to turn around is NOW. If you don't, you'll never get to where you really want to go.

"Study this Book of Instruction continually. Meditate on it day and night so you will be sure to obey everything written in it. Only then will you prosper and succeed in all you do.